SAMUEL F. B. MORSE'S

Gallery of the Louvre

A GUIDE
TO THE PAINTING

SAMUEL F. B. MORSE'S

Gallery of the Louvre

A GUIDE
TO THE PAINTING

Peter John Brownlee

TERRA FOUNDATION FOR AMERICAN ART

Contents

Director's Foreword

SAMUEL F. B. MORSE began his career as a painter. His monumental *Gallery of the Louvre* was the culmination of an extended period of study in Europe. Upon his return to the United States, Morse exhibited the work only twice, in New York and New Haven, where it was praised by critics and connoisseurs but rejected by the public. Crushed by the response, Morse soon ceased painting altogether, moving on to his more successful experiments in communications technology. It would take nearly 150 years for the painting to assume its place as an icon of early American art.

Chicago businessman Daniel J. Terra made his fortune in printing inks and photographic chemicals. He began collecting art as early as 1937, then turned his focus to collecting the art of the United States around 1976, inspired in part by the bicentennial of the nation's independence. In 1982 Terra grabbed the attention of the art world when he purchased Samuel F. B. Morse's *Gallery of the Louvre* for $3.25 million, at the time a record for an American painting. To Mr. Terra, *Gallery of the Louvre* epitomized the American spirit of vitality, initiative, and drive for self-improvement. He immediately sent it on an extended tour of museums across the United States, attracting widespread acclaim that helped reestablish the importance of Morse's painting for the study of early American art history. In that spirit, the Terra Foundation has continued to research and exhibit the painting, which serves as a cornerstone of the Foundation's renowned collection of historical art of the United States, dating from the colonial period to 1950.

The painting underwent an extensive conservation treatment in 2010–11, a process documented in the award-winning documentary, *A New Look: Samuel F. B. Morse's "Gallery of the Louvre,"* produced by Sandpail Productions. Following the treatment, the painting went back on tour for a series of extended exhibitions at the Yale University Art Gallery, the National Gallery of Art, and the Pennsylvania Academy of the Fine Arts, where it was the subject of an extensive array of public lectures, teacher programs, copying classes for practicing artists, and scholarly study days and symposia.

We thank our colleagues at these institutions for their collaboration in the exhibition of the painting and especially for their work in developing the innovative and engaging programs that yielded new insights and advanced scholarly research on the painting. Indeed, the institutional collaboration, deep research, and international dialogue that animate the exhibition and study of Morse's painting reflect the Foundation's belief that art has the power to distinguish cultures as well as to unite them.

As *Gallery of the Louvre* embarks on another extended tour of museums across the United States and beyond, we look forward to sharing the painting with museum audiences and the dialogue and exchange that it inspires.

ELIZABETH GLASSMAN
PRESIDENT AND CHIEF EXECUTIVE OFFICER
TERRA FOUNDATION FOR AMERICAN ART

Acknowledgments

THIS PROJECT BEGAN in earnest with the extensive conservation treatment of *Gallery of the Louvre* undertaken by Lance Mayer and Gay Myers beginning in late 2010. Research for this treatment, and a video documentary of the painting and its conservation produced by Sandpail Productions, formed the basis for the exhibition, *A New Look: Samuel F. B. Morse's "Gallery of the Louvre."*

Our sincere thanks go to everyone at the Yale University Art Gallery, the National Gallery of Art, and the Pennsylvania Academy of the Fine Arts, who helped to realize the special installation of the exhibition and all its attendant programs and publications.

A series of study days and symposia held at these institutions yielded new insights into Morse's painting and shed new light on his complex persona as an erudite artist, scientist, inventor, deeply spiritual Calvinist, and political xenophobe. These findings have been gathered in the multi-authored book *Samuel F. B. Morse's "Gallery of the Louvre" and the Art of Invention* (Chicago: Terra Foundation for American Art, distributed by Yale University Press, 2014).

Thanks to everyone at the Terra Foundation for American Art who collaborated on and lent support to the project. We would also like to thank Michael Tropea for post-conservation photography of the painting and our colleagues at Marquand Books, especially Ed Marquand, Adrian Lucia, Jeff Wincapaw, Gina Glascock-Broze, Ryan Polich, and Melissa Duffes.

PETER JOHN BROWNLEE, ASSOCIATE CURATOR
TERRA FOUNDATION FOR AMERICAN ART

Samuel F. B. Morse's
Gallery of the Louvre

A GUIDE TO THE PAINTING

PETER JOHN BROWNLEE

IN NOVEMBER 1829, Samuel F. B. Morse (fig. 1) boarded a ship bound for London, the first stop on what would become a nearly three-year tour of England, Italy, and France. He was at the height of his artistic powers. Still reeling from the premature death of his beloved wife, Lucretia Pickering Walker Morse, as well as the loss of both his parents, and still struggling to secure his reputation as a great American artist, Morse embarked on a period of intense study and prodigious copying that culminated in his grand *Gallery of the Louvre*. The picture, which measures approximately six feet by nine, depicts an imagined installation of artworks in the Salon Carré at the Musée du Louvre in Paris, compressing thirty-eight paintings, two sculptures, and numerous figures into a single composition. Morse's selection of old master paintings was guided by the teachings of his mentors Washington Allston and Benjamin West and by his own pedagogical aims as president and professor of painting at the National Academy of Design in New York, which he helped to form in 1825–26; it also reflects the taste of his American patrons and peers. But in addition, his strategic arrangement of pictures effectively demonstrates various approaches to the treatment of color, light, line, and composition that exemplified for Morse the capacity of the fine art of painting to reproduce the intellectually stimulating effects of natural phenomena. These he addressed in his famed *Lectures on the Affinity of Painting with the Other Fine Arts*, first delivered at the New York Athenaeum in the spring of 1826.

In the first of his four lectures, Morse claimed that the "principal intention" of the fine arts—painting, sculpture, music, poetry, landscape gardening, oratory, and theater—"is to please the Imagination."[1] In the second lecture he explained that "all the Fine Arts refer to Nature as the source whence they draw their materials, and the Imitation of Nature is always recommended to the student in any of these Arts." But Morse was careful to parse two variants of the imitation so fundamental to reproducing these phenomena, and their effects, in the fine arts. "There is then an Imitation which copies exactly what it sees, makes no selections, no combinations, and there is an Imitation which perceives principles, and arranges its materials according to these principles, so as to produce a desired effect. The first may be called *Mechanical* and the last *Intellectual Imitation*."[2] As an assemblage of copies artfully arranged to produce certain desired effects, *Gallery of the Louvre* involves both, with a decided emphasis on the latter.

In the second lecture Morse also explained the "universal principle" of "connexion."[3] His "Salon style" arrangement of pictures in *Gallery of the Louvre*, like his artistic outlook and general worldview, was clearly guided by selection, recombination, and connectivity. *Gallery of the Louvre* fuses the adoration and imitation of the old masters and the experimental techniques favored by the English painter Joshua Reynolds, as well as by West and Allston, with a genre of gallery paintings that were premised on the relational mode of exhibiting pictures. Intended to highlight stylistic similarities or to emphasize formal or thematic

FIG. 1 Louis-Jacques-Mandé Daguerre (French, 1781–1851). *Samuel Finley Breese Morse*, 1840. Photographic print on board, print: 4¾ × 3¼ in. (12 × 8 cm); board: 5½ × 4 in. (14 × 10 cm). Macbeth Gallery records, Archives of American Art, Smithsonian Institution, Washington, D.C. (DSI-AAA) 2880

relationships, this mode of display was founded on seventeenth-century art theory and typified the Louvre's installations prior to its rearrangement by national school in the late eighteenth century. Instead of simply selecting and arranging what he considered to be the most exemplary and artistically significant pictures in the Louvre's collection, a claim standard to the critical literature on the painting, Morse made his choices according to specific practical and theoretical formulations that he had developed over approximately twenty years, from his early training in London to his ascendancy as an artist of considerable renown.

The period between the end of the War of 1812—when Morse was an aspiring artist in London—and the early 1830s, when the seasoned painter completed *Gallery of the Louvre*, witnessed extensive political, economic, technological, and cultural change in the United States. Territorial expansion, a vast influx of Irish and German immigrants, the relocation of Native Americans from eastern woodlands to western plains, and the ascendancy of Andrew Jackson, the nation's seventh president, altered the character of the nation. The technology of interchangeable parts invented by Eli Whitney and others revolutionized industrial manufacturing. In 1825 the opening of the Erie Canal connected the western hinterlands with trading centers in the East, establishing New York as the nation's new economic and cultural capital. The building of canals, turnpikes, and roads, plus the development of steam-powered ships and early forms of the railroad, collapsed distances and facilitated the flow of agricultural and machine-made goods as well as people and information in various forms. Though the nation remained largely agricultural until the dawn of the twentieth century, immigration and urbanization increased the size and density of America's cities. Developments in papermaking and printing technology facilitated the publication and dissemination of newspapers, periodicals, pamphlets, and books. And major cities saw the gradual establishment of fine art galleries and art organizations such as the American Academy of the Fine Arts, the National Academy of Design, and later the American Art-Union, which cultivated a growing public for fine art prints, paintings, and sculpture. It is easy to see how this flowering of culture, technology, and commerce made conditions ripe for the introduction of Morse's electromagnetic telegraph in 1844. But these interrelated developments also made a painting like *Gallery of the Louvre* possible, if not entirely probable—nor, as Morse would learn to his chagrin, profitable.[4]

Simultaneously engaged in artistic, scientific, technological, and even political pursuits throughout this period, Morse demonstrated a capacity for associative thinking and a propensity for carrying out thought in action across multiple forms. These various strands of his complex intellect have attracted the attention of generations of scholars who have maintained that the artist constructed *Gallery of the Louvre* to serve as an instrument for teaching and as a vehicle for improving cultural awareness and aesthetic taste in the United States. Specifically how the painting carried out this work has been left relatively unexamined. Biographers in the mid-twentieth century hailed Morse as the "American Leonardo" and later as America's "lightning man."[5] Art historian Paul Staiti's exhaustive critical biography remains the most comprehensive study of the artist and inventor.[6] Staiti's Morse is an eighteenth-century intellectual thoroughly embedded in a nineteenth-century world and an adamant, if conflicted, champion of American cultural nationalism. Taking the *Kunstkammer* and the gallery picture as his points of departure in creating *Gallery of the Louvre*, Morse, as Staiti notes, transformed those elite genres into a demonstration of democratic access to the highest forms of culture.[7]

However, as Staiti also asserts, Morse approached democracy and the cultural "others" who exercised it with a suspicion that often freighted, and thus compromised, the egalitarian aspects of his cultural output.[8] Though his readiness to experiment and innovate continued throughout his career, Morse became ever more outspoken in his cultural conservatism. He painted *Gallery of the Louvre* during the same period in which he completed the manuscript for *Foreign Conspiracy against the Liberties of the United States* (1835), the first of several diatribes against what he saw as the contagion of foreign influence, particularly those elements associated with the pope and the Catholic Church.[9] The painting has been interpreted as a compilation of scenes divested of their overtly Catholic subject matter, first by the secularizing effects of Napoleonic plunder and second by Morse's aestheticization of them in his painting. Setting aside their religious content, as some have proposed, Morse's emphasis on the potential

of these masterpieces of Renaissance and Baroque painting to enlighten his fellow Americans and to raise the standard of cultural taste in his native country accorded with the artist's strongly Calvinist faith.[10]

Other scholars have examined the painting in relation to the study of natural history or to the vogue for single-painting exhibitions and related forms of visual entertainment, such as the moving panorama. Others have located in the painting the seeds of Morse's experiments with the daguerreotype, the electromagnetic telegraph, and Morse code.[11] Indeed, the painting culminates Morse's ascent as a fine artist, emblematizes his transition from painter to inventor, and exemplifies the hybrid complexity of this thinking. However, the painting's poor public reception demonstrates the artist's failure to connect with his intended audience. Though underappreciated in its time, *Gallery of the Louvre* embodies an intersection of art, religion, science, and technology. Thoroughly of its cultural moment, the painting continues to invite and reward divergent yet interrelated lines of speculation and study regarding its conception, design, and execution.

MORSE'S EARLY CAREER

Born in Charlestown, Massachusetts, on April 27, 1791, to Jedidiah Morse—a Congregational minister and a geographer—and Elizabeth Ann Finley Breese Morse, Samuel Finley Breese Morse grew up with the young nation, and came to embody its great intellectual and artistic promise as well as its many ideological contradictions. His worldview was shaped by Calvinism and by the millennialist belief that the founding of the United States of America was divinely predestined to initiate a thousand years of peace; by his academic and scientific training under the scientist Benjamin Silliman, the Reverend Timothy Dwight, and others at Yale University; and by his artistic training under the tutelage of Allston, whom the young

FIG. 2 Washington Allston (American, 1779–1843). *Self-Portrait*, 1805. Oil on canvas, 31⅝ × 26½ in. (80.3 × 67.3 cm). Museum of Fine Arts, Boston

FIG. 3 Sir Thomas Lawrence (English, 1769–1830). *Portrait of Benjamin West*, 1818–21. Oil on canvas, 107 × 69½ in. (271.1 × 176.5 cm). Purchased by subscription, Wadsworth Atheneum, Hartford, Connecticut, 1855.1

Morse first met in Boston in 1810 (fig. 2). The episteme into which Morse emerged as a young scholar and artist was framed by the Enlightenment thinking of previous generations and structured by a belief in an ordered universe and a stable social hierarchy led by a patrician elite.

As a young man, Morse devoted his many talents to becoming a fine artist. On July 13, 1811, he sailed for London, where he joined Allston and a circle of American artists that included John Singleton Copley, Benjamin West, and John Trumbull, as well as the British painter Charles Robert Leslie, who quickly became Morse's constant companion. On the strength of a drawing that Morse made after a plaster cast of the *Laocoön*, he was admitted to the Royal Academy of Arts. The Academy's first president, Joshua Reynolds, set the terms for artistic theory and practice in his *Discourses on Art* (delivered as lectures to Academy students between 1769 and 1790) and by the example of his painting, which manifested his preference for the Italian Renaissance, his notions of artistic imitation, and his predilection for experimental media and techniques.[12] The model set forth by Reynolds was elaborated by his successor as president, Benjamin West, a painter of grand manner history paintings who is depicted lecturing on color in Sir Thomas Lawrence's portrait (fig. 3). Reynolds, West, and others at the Academy stressed the importance of innovation in the painting of erudite subjects and technical prowess that included accurate anatomical drawing and proper perspective as well as the ability to re-create the look and feel of old master paintings. Morse's official program of study in London was dictated by West and the methods of the Academy but overseen by Allston, who served as his private master.[13]

12

Morse's first major painting at the Academy, *Dying Hercules* (fig. 4), exhibited in 1813, won him critical acclaim and clearly demonstrates how thoroughly he had absorbed the Academy's mandates under Allston's guiding hand. The reclining figure echoes that of the *Laocoön*, but the painting was, more pointedly, a direct response to Allston's *Dead Man Restored to Life by Touching the Bones of the Prophet Elisha* (fig. 5), completed while Morse was laboring on his *Hercules*. Though focused on a single figure, Morse's painting adopts the vertical format of *Dead Man Restored to Life* and reflects Allston's interest in anatomy as well as physiology, as seen most vividly in their depictions of the transformation of the flesh—from death to life in Allston's picture and from life to death in Morse's. Reanimation was a topic of much scientific and cultural debate at the time, with several scientists extolling the potential of the galvanic battery for that purpose. After all, these were the years that witnessed the birth of the monster in Mary Shelley's *Frankenstein* (1818).[14]

Buoyed by his success in London, Morse returned home in 1815 to a cultural climate not favorably disposed to grand manner history paintings. In 1818 he married Lucretia Pickering Walker, with whom he would have three children in the seven years before her death. Morse had written to his parents from London, informing them of his ambition "to be among those who shall revive the splendour of the 15th century, to rival the genius of a Raphael, a Michael Angelo, or a Titian." But his wish "to shine, not by a light borrowed from them, but to strive to shine the brightest" was not to be, or at least not in the form he anticipated at this early stage of his career.[15] Instead, like other painters of his generation, he was

FIG. 4 Samuel F. B. Morse. *Dying Hercules*, 1812–13. Oil on canvas, 96¼ × 78⅛ in. (239.4 × 198.3 cm). Gift of the artist, Yale University Art Gallery, 1866.3

FIG. 5 Washington Allston (American, 1779–1843). *Dead Man Restored to Life by Touching the Bones of the Prophet Elisha*, 1811–13. Oil on canvas, 156 × 122 in. (396.2 × 309.9 cm). Purchase, by subscription, Pennsylvania Academy of the Fine Arts, Philadelphia, 1816.1

forced to turn to portrait painting for financial support. During much of this period, Morse traveled up and down the Eastern Seaboard, painting portraits in Boston, New York, Washington, D.C., and Charleston, South Carolina, where he also helped establish the short-lived South Carolina Academy of Fine Arts—a forerunner to his more successful efforts in founding the National Academy of Design in New York a few years later. Though he often lamented the lack of taste in his home country and expressed doubts about his chosen profession, Morse persisted. His portraits from this period clearly evince an evolving talent.

Morse's experience as a portraitist and his desire to advance a strong and elevated national art came together in *The House of Representatives* (fig. 6). Compiling nearly one hundred portraits of congressmen, delegates, and other figures painted from life, the painting is a grand and complex picture. Morse arrived in Washington in November 1821 and set up a studio adjacent to the House floor, where he spent nearly four months painting portraits of the various individuals he would eventually include in his mammoth canvas. He finally completed the painting in January 1823 and sent it directly to Boston for display, the first stop on an ill-fated tour that also included exhibition venues in Manhattan and Albany, New York; Hartford and Middletown, Connecticut; and Springfield and Northampton, Massachusetts. Morse sought to capitalize on popular interest in the grand revolutionary scenes painted by John Trumbull for the Capitol Rotunda and in the spectacular pestilence and plague of Rembrandt Peale's *The Court of Death* (1820; Detroit Institute of Arts). Lacking the pictorial and narrative drama that attracted crowds to these and other single-painting exhibitions, *The House of Representatives* was a commercial failure and attracted only modest notice in the press. Disappointed, Morse abandoned the tour and shipped his rolled canvas to Charles Robert Leslie in London, who attempted to sell the painting for his old friend.[16] Morse had miscalculated the interests of a public more inclined to favor mummies, circuses, and minstrel shows. It would not be his last such miscalculation.

Out of necessity, Morse returned to portraiture, painting in New Haven, New York, and elsewhere in a desperate attempt to support his family while continuing his chosen profession. One commission led to another, forcing him to return to the itinerancy he loathed. The paired portraits of David Curtis DeForest and his wife, Julia Wooster DeForest (1823; The Yale University Art Gallery), exemplify the series of pendants Morse executed during the 1820s, which are some of the finest and most accomplished paintings of his entire career. In spite of the prosaic nature of such portraiture, he still found opportunities for technical experimentation: for example, for his exquisite portrait of his wife, Lucretia, and their two oldest children, Susan and Charles, he ground his pigments with milk, which perhaps contributed to the picture's pearly quality (1824; High Museum of Art).

Returning to New York from another extended period of itinerancy in November 1824, Morse bested a group of competitors that included Henry Inman, Rembrandt Peale, Thomas Sully, and John Vanderlyn, among others, winning a prized commission from the City of New York to paint a full-length portrait of the Revolutionary War hero the Marquis de Lafayette, who was then at the beginning of his triumphal "farewell" tour of the United States. The prestige of this commission revitalized Morse, but his enthusiasm was overshadowed by the news that Lucretia, then recovering from the birth of their third child, Finley, had died unexpectedly. Still mourning his wife, Morse busied himself with painting the full-length portrait of Lafayette (1825–26; Art Commission of the City of New York, City Hall) during the early part of 1826, while also devoting a significant portion of his time to establishing the National Academy of Design in New York.

FIG. 6 Samuel F. B. Morse. *The House of Representatives*, completed 1822, probably reworked 1823. Oil on canvas, 86⅞ × 130⅝ in. (220.6 × 331.8 cm). Corcoran Gallery of Art, Washington, D.C.

MORSE AND THE ACADEMY

Modeled on London's Royal Academy, which Morse had experienced firsthand, the National Academy of Design was formed to provide instruction for American artists and a space for the annual exhibition of their work. Morse served the Academy as president and professor from 1826 to 1845 (a tenure interrupted only by his resignation to travel abroad between late 1829 and 1832). He immediately set to work on a program of lectures that would outline the need for such an institution and articulate its founding principles, as well as communicate his persistent ambition to advance a national art. In late March and early April 1826, Morse delivered four lectures at the New York Athenaeum, presented in tandem with a series of four talks on poetry by

William Cullen Bryant. Professing affinity between a steam engine and "a page of verse, the sounds of an instrument, a colored canvas, a pile of buildings, a statue, and a decorated pleasure ground," Morse laid out a set of principles for his own synthesizing artistic practice, one that embraced "the arts of design" as well as the science of art.[17] These lectures, reflective of his particular turn of mind and his absorption of the ideas and practices of Reynolds, Allston, and Silliman, among others, would eventually provide a blueprint for *Gallery of the Louvre*.

With the elevated goal of stimulating the imagination, Morse's *Lectures* exemplified the "intellectual imitation" derived from careful observation, astute selection, and calculated recombination that formed the basis for his intellectual and artistic output. He had deployed these principles in composing *Dying Hercules*, and he returned to them in crafting the lectures, which drew on sources ranging from Aristotle's *Poetics* and the journals of Leonardo da Vinci to the *Discourses* of Reynolds and West. Morse's combination of ideas selected from these and other philosophers and artists, both ancient and modern, gave the *Lectures* novelty as well as intellectual heft.

Morse labored over the lectures for months. Perhaps this process illuminated the need to deepen his knowledge of the finest European collections of art, to gather treatises and prints that would be useful to Academy students, and

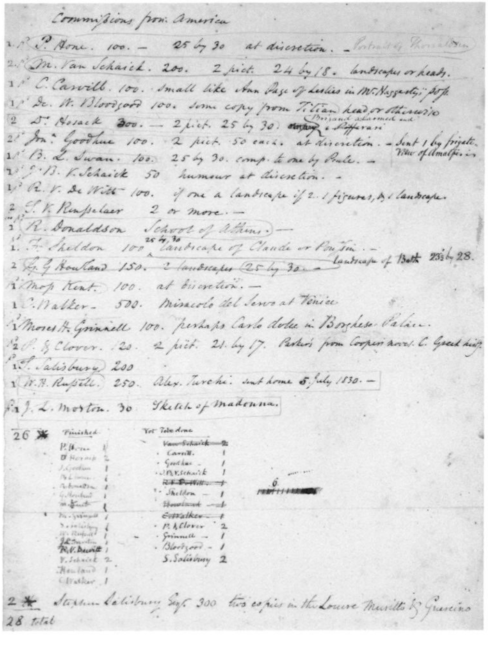

FIG. 7 Samuel F. B. Morse. List of Commissions, general correspondence bound volume, 11 Feb 1828–13 July 1832, image 194. Samuel F. B. Morse Papers, 1793–1944, Library of Congress, Washington, D.C., Manuscript Division

to hone his skills as a painter and colorist by copying works of great significance. (In his fourth lecture on painting, Morse apologized for having to illustrate his points with black-and-white engravings after old master paintings.)[18] In the fall of 1829 he again traversed the Atlantic to spend an extended period in England, Italy, and France in order to increase his knowledge of the western tradition and to improve his mastery of painting through close study and careful copying. He hoped that these pursuits, in addition to being entirely appropriate for the president of the National Academy of Design, would also prepare him for the commission he had long sought: to execute a mural painting in the Capitol Rotunda, a project that he hoped would finally establish him as one of America's preeminent artists. (That commission would never come to pass.) He underwrote the trip with commissions from collectors and art patrons such as Stephen Salisbury of central Massachusetts and Robert Donaldson of North Carolina for copies of old master works (fig. 7). These men were eager for copies of often-unspecified paintings by Raphael, Bartholomé Esteban Murillo, or Nicolas Poussin. For Charles Walker, Morse's brother-in-law, the artist painted a scaled-down copy of Jacopo Tintoretto's *Miracle of Saint Mark* (1548; Gallerie dell'Accademia, Venice); other than pencil sketches, this is the only copy from the list known to be extant. These commissions may have been influenced by Morse's lectures, since these were among the artists he discussed and illustrated. Perhaps he anticipated that these copies, or others like them, would not only help fund his travel and give him important lessons in composition and coloring but also prove useful for illustrating future lectures.

Morse embarked for London in late 1829 and passed through Paris early the next year, when he made a brief visit to the Louvre and noted several pictures he intended to copy upon his return to Paris. This was followed by an extended stay in Italy, where he studied and sketched in the finest collections for over a year. Morse's diaries record visits to the Vatican, where he obtained permission to copy works by Salvator Rosa and others; to the Borghese and Doria palaces; and to private and public galleries in Rome, Florence, and Milan, where he studied and sometimes copied works by Leonardo, Claude Lorrain, Raphael, Titian, and Veronese. Morse filled his sketchbooks with notes and drawings documenting the paintings he saw, with extensive annotations indicating colors and other details relevant to the production of full-color copies.[19] His pencil sketches illustrate his system of shorthand notation of a painting's hues and saturations. Full of comments regarding strong examples of rich coloring or fine drawing, excellent composition or dramatic expression, Morse's travel diaries and sketchbooks document his activities and impressions. Together with the canon of the greatest masters of the sixteenth and seventeenth centuries instilled in him by his mentors, plus the list of commissions underwriting his trip, they helped shape the agenda for his time at the Louvre.

COMPOSING *GALLERY OF THE LOUVRE*

Morse returned to Paris in September 1831 and quickly fell in with James Fenimore Cooper (fig. 8), already the celebrated American author of *The Pioneers* (1823) and *The Last of the Mohicans* (1826), whom Morse had come to know as a member of the Bread and Cheese Club, a literary and artistic circle established in New York in 1824. They found Paris reeling from the revolution of the previous year, and they were swept up in the fervor of the July Monarchy—a topic that preoccupied Morse and his Paris cohort, which included Cooper, the sculptor Horatio Greenough, and the landscape painter Thomas Cole. In addition, a cholera epidemic was sweeping the city, forcing officials to pile corpses in the streets—a grisly detail reported by Morse in his letters back home.[20] These events, along with Morse's increasingly xenophobic critique

of what he saw as the excesses of Catholic Europe, formed the backdrop for his creation of *Gallery of the Louvre*. As president and professor of painting at the National Academy of Design, Morse may have selected and arranged the artworks in his grand composition primarily to offer lessons in composition, chiaroscuro, and coloring. But other factors were certainly at play.

Compiling his selections from the Louvre—the most dazzling and comprehensive collection in Europe—into a single canvas posed numerous challenges. Morse worked diligently to depict the relatively compact space of the Salon Carré in proper perspective, which was critical to the efficacy of his design. To help him render this grand architectural space in two dimensions, Morse likely employed a camera obscura or other such mechanical

FIG. 8 John Wesley Jarvis (American, 1781–1840). *James Fenimore Cooper*, 1822. Oil on canvas, 30 × 25 in. (76.2 × 63.5 cm). Fenimore Art Museum, Cooperstown/The New York Historical Society, N0146.1977

device, as he had in composing *The House of Representatives*.[21] To introduce greater depth into the composition, and to offer respite for the eyes from so many pictures to see, Morse situated his composition on the vertical axis of the entrance into the Grande Galerie, where several of his selections would actually have been hanging. Enabling a recession into space denied by the Salon's strict square ("*carré*"), the rectangle of the open doorway into the Grand Galerie—grandly scaled and dotted with figures strolling and admiring works of art throughout the elongated hall—can almost be read as if it were another painting.

Morse's conception of his gallery picture necessitated careful thought regarding which pictures to include and numerous calculations for artfully scaling and arranging them. *Gallery of the Louvre* takes liberties with the scale of most, if not all, of its pictures.[22] To carry out his work at the Louvre, Morse positioned himself in front of his chosen masterworks; he either painted them directly into his large canvas or made scaled-down sketches and finished copies on smaller supports, like that of *Francis I* (fig. 9). The discovery by the conservators Lance Mayer and Gay Myers of tiny pinholes at the corners of Veronese's *Christ Carrying the Cross*, just to the right of the doorway, suggests that in addition to rendering his copies directly onto a designated portion of his canvas, Morse also made sketches of individual works on bits of paper or other malleable surface and pinned these in place to test their fit and determine their *part* to the painting's *whole*.[23]

Working assiduously, with breaks only to eat and sleep, Morse completed most of the painting—the architecture and the pictures—in Paris; he did not finish the figures populating the gallery or the frames on the pictures until after returning to New York. He boasted in a letter to his brothers, "It is a great labor but it will be a splendid and valuable work, it excites a great deal of attention from strangers and the French artists, I have many compliments upon it. I am sure it is the most *correct* of *its kind* ever

FIG. 9 Samuel F. B. Morse. *Francis I, Study for "Gallery of the Louvre"*, 1831–33. Oil on panel, 10 × 8 in. (25.4 × 20.3 cm). Copy after Titian. Gift of Berry-Hill Galleries in honor of Daniel J. Terra. Terra Foundation for American Art, Chicago, C1984.5

painted, for every one says I have caught the style of each of the masters."[24] Racing to finish the painting prior to the Louvre's annual closure in August, Morse blended varnishes into his pigment mixtures to enhance the old master qualities of his painting as well as to quicken the drying process. He rolled his canvas and set sail for home in October 1832. Not until unrolling the canvas in early 1833, intending to finally finish it, did Morse discover the damage caused by his materials and techniques. His attempts at repair often caused even more harm. For example, he undertook some hasty measures to fix certain passages of damage in the coat of his self-portrait at center; in that of the copyist at left, thought to be Morse's friend Richard West Habersham; and in several other passages throughout the composition, including losses in the lower portion of the wall at right.

Upon its completion, Morse exhibited the painting in a rented second-floor room at the corner of Broadway and Pine Street in Manhattan in the fall of 1833. He also produced a catalogue that included a description of the Louvre's extensive collections, a brief narrative of his own project, and an annotated key to the painting. Though *Gallery of the Louvre* drew praise from critics and connoisseurs, it failed to attract a popular audience.[25] And so Morse sent the painting on to New Haven, where its lackluster performance was repeated. It is thought that during their time together in Paris, Cooper had agreed to buy the painting directly from Morse, an arrangement perhaps corroborated by the discovery of the pencil inscription "Co" in the skirt of the seated figure in the group that has long been identified as the Cooper family. But this did not come to pass. Following its disappointing reception in New Haven, Morse sold the painting and its frame to George Hyde Clarke, a relative of Cooper's whose portrait Morse had painted in 1829 overlooking Hyde Hall, his manor on the northwestern shore of Otsego Lake (1829; Saint Louis Art Museum). As part of their negotiations, Morse offered to paint in the figures of Clarke and his family—presumably in place of the Coopers—but Clarke apparently declined. The painting hung for a time at Hyde Hall and descended through the Clarke family until 1884, when it was placed on long-term loan at Syracuse University; in 1892 it entered the institution's collection. In 1982 the Chicago businessman and collector Daniel J. Terra purchased the painting for a then-record sum and sent it on an extended tour, grander than Morse could ever have envisioned. A decade later the painting became part of the collection of the Terra Foundation for American Art, which exhibits it regularly in museums in the United States and abroad in order to advance the Foundation's mission of bringing American art to the world and the world to American art.

THE ACHIEVEMENT OF *GALLERY OF THE LOUVRE*

Despite being eclipsed initially by its failure to connect with audiences, *Gallery of the Louvre* remains a grand achievement of great complexity. The compositional design and conceptual underpinnings of the picture were made clearer by the extensive conservation treatment of 2010–11.[26] Elements of Morse's pedagogical program may be traced in his strategic placement of artworks throughout the composition, which collectively emphasize the dialogic nature of the painting. Though the reasons for his selection and arrangement of these specific pictures are not documented, compelling clues to the artist's intentions are evident in his 1826 *Lectures*. In them, Morse constructed an idealized viewer and a manner of viewing the complicated picture he would execute a few years later. Morse's selection of individual pictures as examples of strong design or color, of contrast or gradation, demonstrates his erudition, while the overall assemblage exemplifies his use of intellectual imitation to combine individual components—in this case, old master paintings—into a harmonious and instructive whole. These various components, which he carefully selected for their individual characteristics as well as for their complex interrelationships, reflect the theoretical underpinnings of *Gallery of the Louvre* and contribute to its compositional unity. Morse cited the example of the steam engine, in which the various valves and levers, in spite of their diversity, "all unite to produce one result."[27] As a tightly orchestrated constellation of pictorial components, *Gallery of the Louvre* illustrates the same point.

Like the identity of the various figures he included, Morse's intentions in painting *Gallery of the Louvre* are not entirely known. But the overriding sense of connection that links his major works encourages us to think they were developed as instrumental parts of a greater whole.

FIG. 10 Samuel F. B. Morse. "Canvas Stretcher" telegraph, 1837. Record unit 95, box 41, folder 1, 91-3689. Division of Work & Industry, National Museum of American History, Smithsonian Institution

Indeed, if Morse's *Lectures* provided a kind of blueprint for the construction of *Gallery of the Louvre*, as I have suggested, the painting itself provided intellectual and material scaffolding for the conceptualization of his next great invention. Not only did Morse utilize a canvas stretcher in building an early prototype of his telegraphic transmitter (fig. 10), he also employed the artists' material asphaltum, combined with linseed oil and turpentine, to coat and protect his conductor wire.[28] Painters such as Allston and his student Morse added this brown, tarlike substance to their pigment mixtures in order to give their paintings the antique look of the old masters. But asphaltum could be quite volatile, causing colors to darken rapidly or damaging a painting's surface as it dried. It was likely the agent responsible for the bubbling and cracking seen throughout the entire left side of Morse's painting. Thus, the same material that may have helped give Morse's copies the look and feel of old master paintings was, ironically, both a

detriment to his canvas and a protective element for his telegraphic wires.

In more ways than one, Morse's grand painting, a picture filled with copies and copyists, exemplifies his unique art of invention rather than mere imitation—a complex "engine" of carefully calibrated interrelated parts. Created in a period of intense economic and technological development, *Gallery of the Louvre* marries old master techniques and the tenets of European art history with New World ingenuity. Wedding his vast erudition and intellectual prowess to mechanical skill and creative invention, Morse sought to capitalize on Americans' lack of familiarity with the old masters and their taste for visual entertainments such as popular single-painting exhibitions and panoramas. Though an acolyte of Reynolds, West, and especially Allston, Morse was also a student of Robert Fulton, Silliman, and other men of science and technological innovation. The classrooms and laboratories of Yale University; Allston's Boston studio; the lecture halls, ateliers, and exhibition spaces of London's Royal Academy as well as those of the newly formed National Academy of Design; and the great galleries of the Louvre all became part of his intellectual matrix for bringing together the mechanics of the universe with the manipulations of art. However, as articulate as Morse could be in his writings, he never fully spelled out the connections linking his written and his visual productions, leaving scholars to ponder his intentions and the complex formulas involved in creating *Gallery of the Louvre*.

Notes

1 Samuel F. B. Morse, *Lectures on the Affinity of Painting with the Other Fine Arts*, ed. Nicolai Cikovsky, Jr. (Columbia: University of Missouri Press, 1983), 49. Also instructive are Morse's working notes made in preparation for the *Lectures*, now housed in the Samuel F. B. Morse Papers, Academy Archives, National Academy of Design, New York.

2 Ibid., 58–59.

3 Ibid., 63.

4 Daniel Walker Howe, *What Hath God Wrought: The Transformation of America, 1815–1848* (New York: Oxford University Press, 2007); and Charles Sellers, *The Market Revolution: Jacksonian America, 1815–1846* (New York: Oxford University Press, 1994).

5 Carlton Mabee, *The American Leonardo: A Life of Samuel F. B. Morse* (New York: Alfred A. Knopf, 1943); Kenneth Silverman, *Lightning Man: The Accursed Life of Samuel F. B. Morse* (New York: Alfred A. Knopf, 2003). Another biography of note is William Kloss, *Samuel F. B. Morse* (New York: Harry N. Abrams in association with the National Museum of American Art, Smithsonian Institution, 1988). Morse's time in Paris forms the subject of two chapters in historian David McCullough's *The Greater Journey: Americans in Paris* (New York: Simon and Schuster, 2011).

6 Paul J. Staiti, *Samuel F. B. Morse* (Cambridge: Cambridge University Press, 1989).

7 Ibid., 236–37.

8 Ibid., 191–93.

9 *Foreign Conspiracy against the Liberties of the United States: The Numbers of Brutus, Originally Published in the "New-York Observer"* (New York: Leavitt, Lord, 1835).

10 Patricia Johnston, "Samuel F. B. Morse's *Gallery of the Louvre*: Social Tensions in an Ideal World," in *Seeing High and Low: Representing Social Conflict in American Visual Culture*, ed. Patricia Johnston (Berkeley: University of California Press, 2006), 42–65.

11 Rachael DeLue, Tanya Pohrt, Sarah Kate Gillespie, Jean-Philippe Antoine, and others have examined these aspects of Morse's career in relation to *Gallery of the Louvre*. See *Samuel F. B. Morse's "Gallery of the Louvre" and the Art of Invention*, ed. Peter John Brownlee (Chicago: Terra Foundation for American Art, distributed by Yale University Press, 2014). See also Lisa Gitelman, "Modes and Codes: Samuel F. B. Morse and the Question of Electronic Writing," in *This Is Enlightenment*, ed. Clifford Siskin and William Warner (Chicago: University of Chicago Press, 2010), 120–35.

12 Joshua Reynolds, *Discourses on Art*, 1769–90, ed. Pat Rogers (New York: Penguin Books, 1992).

13 Staiti, *Morse*, 15.

14 While a student at Yale, Morse attended lectures on electricity by Silliman and Jeremiah Day. Ibid., 6.

15 Morse to Jedidiah Morse, May 3, 1815, Samuel F. B. Morse Papers, 1793–1944, Manuscript Division, Library of Congress, Washington, D.C.

16 Leslie tried selling the painting to the art patron George Wyndham, third Earl of Egremont, who was "wholly indifferent to it." See Paul Staiti, *"The House of Representatives,"* in *Corcoran Gallery of Art: American Paintings to 1945*, ed. Sarah Cash (Washington, D.C.: Corcoran Gallery of Art, 2011), 70–71.

17 Morse, *Lectures*, 47.

18 "With respect to the illustrations generally that I am about to use in this lecture, I have to ask the indulgence of my audience. Although they explain the points to be illustrated, yet many of them are so small that I am aware that they can not be seen by all in the room, nor in the hasty selection of examples I was under the necessity of making, could I choose larger. I was compelled to take these as they are or copy them of a proper size, a labor of many months." Morse, *Lectures*, 91–92.

19 Samuel F. B. Morse, Diaries—22 December 1829–3 May 1830; 4 May 1830–3 March 1831; 4 March–31 July 1831; 2 August–12 September 1831; and diary fragments, Samuel F. B. Morse Papers, 1793–1944, Manuscript Division, Library of Congress, Washington, D.C.

20 "I have but a little space to add, that the Cholera is again on the increase in Paris, 100 deaths per day." Morse to Sidney and Richard Morse, July 18, 1832, Samuel F. B. Morse Papers, 1793–1944, Manuscript Division, Library of Congress, Washington, D.C.

21 Staiti, *Morse*, 80.

22 In fact, all copyists were required to resize their reproductions to avoid confusion between copies and originals.

23 On the relation between part and whole, see Morse, *Lectures*, 67–69.

24 Morse to Sidney and Richard Morse, July 18, 1832, Samuel F. B. Morse Papers, 1793–1944, Manuscript Division, Library of Congress, Washington, D.C.

25 "They who were in the room when we first visited it, (and there were many who had been in the Louvre,) spoke in no measured terms of its richness, variety, and correctness. . . . We know not which most to admire, in contemplating this magnificent design, the courage which could undertake such an [sic] herculean task, or the perseverance and success with which it has been completed. We have never seen any thing of this kind before in this country. Its effect on us is different from that made by any other painting." "Mr. Morse's Gallery of the Louvre," *New-York Mirror: A Weekly Gazette of Literature and the Fine Arts* 11 (November 2, 1833): 142.

26 For more on the conservation treatment, see Lance Mayer and Gay Myers, *"Gallery of the Louvre*: Glazing and Problems of Preservation," *Samuel F. B. Morse's "Gallery of the Louvre" and the Art of Invention*, ed. Peter John Brownlee (Chicago: Terra Foundation for American Art, distributed by Yale University Press, 2014), 184–190.

27 Morse, *Lectures*, 62–63.

28 "Morse's Magnetic Telegraph," *Niles' National Register* (Baltimore), June 22, 1844, 261.

A Guide to the Painting

✦ ✦ ✦

Key to the People and Art in Samuel F. B. Morse's *Gallery of the Louvre*

THIS KEY is an updated version of Morse's original catalogue; it reflects current scholarship and includes possible identities of some of the figures.

ART

1 Paolo Caliari, known as Veronese (1528–1588, Italian), *Wedding Feast at Cana*

2 Bartolomé Estebán Murillo (1618–1682, Spanish), *Immaculate Conception*

3 Jean Jouvenet (1644–1717, French), *Descent from the Cross*

4 Jacopo Robusti, known as Tintoretto (1518–1594, Italian), *Self-Portrait*

5 Nicolas Poussin (1594–1665, French), *Deluge (Winter)*

6 Michelangelo Merisi, known as Caravaggio (c. 1571–1610, Italian), *Fortune Teller*

7 Tiziano Vecellio, known as Titian (1488/9–1576, Italian), *Christ Crowned with Thorns*

8 Anthony van Dyck (1599–1641, Flemish), *Venus at the Forge of Vulcan*

9 Claude Gelée, known as Claude Lorrain (c. 1602–1682, French), *Disembarkation of Cleopatra at Tarsus*

10 Bartolomé Estebán Murillo (1618–1682, Spanish), *Holy Family*

11 David Teniers II (1610–1690, Flemish), *Knife Grinder*

12 Rembrandt Harmensz van Rijn (1606–1669, Dutch), *The Angel Leaving the Family of Tobias*

13 Nicolas Poussin (1594–1665, French), *Diogenes Casting Away His Cup*

14 Tiziano Vecellio, known as Titian (1488/9–1576, Italian), *Supper at Emmaus*

15 Cornelis Huysmans (1648–1727, Flemish), *Landscape with Shepherds and Herd*

16 Anthony van Dyck (1599–1641, Flemish), *Portrait of a Lady and Her Daughter*

17 Tiziano Vecellio, known as Titian (1488/9–1576, Italian), *Francis I*

18 Bartolomé Estebán Murillo (1618–1682, Spanish), *Beggar Boy*

19 Paolo Caliari, known as Veronese (1528–1588, Italian), *Christ Carrying the Cross*

20 Leonardo da Vinci (1452–1519, Italian), *Mona Lisa*

21 Antonio Allegri, known as Correggio (c. 1489–1534, Italian), *Mystic Marriage of Saint Catherine of Alexandria with Saint Sebastian*

22 Peter Paul Rubens (1577–1640, Flemish), *Lot and His Family Fleeing Sodom*

23 Claude Gelée, known as Claude Lorrain (c. 1602–1682, French), *Sunset at the Harbor*

24 Tiziano Vecellio, known as Titian (1488/9–1576, Italian), *Entombment*

25 Eustache Le Sueur and his studio (1616–1655, French), *Christ Carrying the Cross*

26 Salvator Rosa (1615–1673, Italian), *Landscape with Soldiers and Hunters*

27 Raffaello Santi, known as Raphael (1483–1520, Italian), *Madonna and Child with the Infant Saint John the Baptist,* called *La Belle Jardinière*

28 Anthony van Dyck (1599–1641, Flemish), *Portrait of a Man in Black* (the artist Paul de Vos?)

29 Guido Reni (1575–1642, Italian), *The Union of Design and Color*

30 Peter Paul Rubens (1577–1640, Flemish), *Portrait of Suzanne Fourment*

31 Simone Cantarini (1612–1648, Italian), *Rest on the Flight into Egypt*

32 Rembrandt Harmensz van Rijn (1606–1669, Dutch), *Head of an Old Man*

33 Anthony van Dyck (1599–1641, Flemish), *Jesus with the Woman Taken in Adultery*

34 Joseph Vernet (1714–1789, French), *Marine View by Moonlight*

35 Guido Reni (1575–1642, Italian), *Deianeira Abducted by the Centaur Nessus*

36 Peter Paul Rubens (1577–1640, Flemish), *Tomyris, Queen of the Scyths*

37 Pierre Mignard (1612–1695, French), *Madonna and Child*

38 Jean-Antoine Watteau (1684–1721, French), *Pilgrimage to the Isle of Cythera*

39 Borghese Vase (1st century BC, Greek)

40 *Artemis with a Doe,* called *Diana of Versailles*. Roman copy after Greek original attributed to Leochares (4th century BC, Greek)

PEOPLE

A Samuel F. B. Morse

B Copyist, possibly a Miss Joreter, who took lessons from Morse at the Louvre, or Susan Walker Morse, daughter of Morse

C James Fenimore Cooper, author and friend of Morse

D Susan DeLancey Cooper, wife of Cooper

E Susan Fenimore Cooper, daughter of James and Susan DeLancey Cooper

F Richard West Habersham, artist and Morse's roommate in Paris

G Horatio Greenough, artist and Morse's roommate in Paris

H Copyist, possibly Morse's recently deceased wife, Lucretia Pickering Walker, or a Miss Joreter

Samuel F. B. Morse (American, 1791–1872). *Gallery of the Louvre*, 1831–33.
Oil on canvas, 73¾ × 108 in. (187.3 × 274.3 cm). Terra Foundation for
American Art, Chicago, Daniel J. Terra Collection, 1992.51

12 Rembrandt Harmensz van Rijn (Dutch, 1606–1669). *The Angel Leaving the Family of Tobias*, 1637. Oil on wood, 26¾ × 20½ in. (68 × 52 cm). Musée du Louvre, Paris, inv. 1736

18 Bartolomé Estebán Murillo (Spanish, 1618–1682). *Beggar Boy*, ca. 1648. Oil on canvas, 53¹⁵⁄₁₆ × 45¼ in. (137 × 115 cm). Musée du Louvre, Paris, no. 933

10 Bartolomé Esteban Murillo: (Spanish, 1618–1682). *Holy Family*,
also called the *Virgin of Seville*, 1665–70. Oil on canvas, 94½ × 74¹³⁄₁₆ in.
(240 × 190 cm). Musée du Louvre, Paris

9 Claude Lorrain (French, ca. 1602–1682). *Disembarkation of Cleopatra at Tarsus*, 1642–43. Oil on canvas, 46⅞ × 66⅛ in. (119 × 168 cm). Musée du Louvre, Paris

14 Titian (Italian, 1488/89–1576). *Supper at Emmaus*, ca. 1530. Oil on canvas, 69⅟₁₆ × 96⅟₁₆ in. (169 × 244 cm). Musée du Louvre, Paris

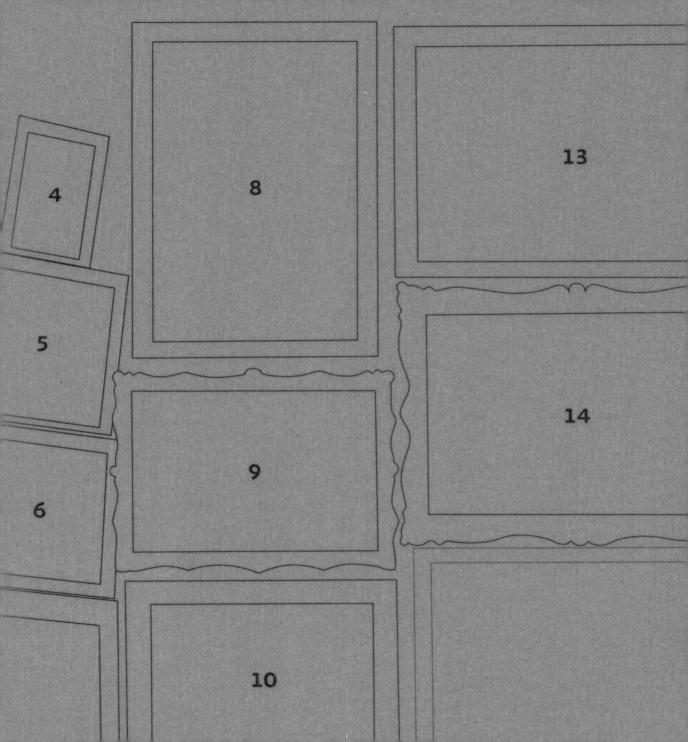

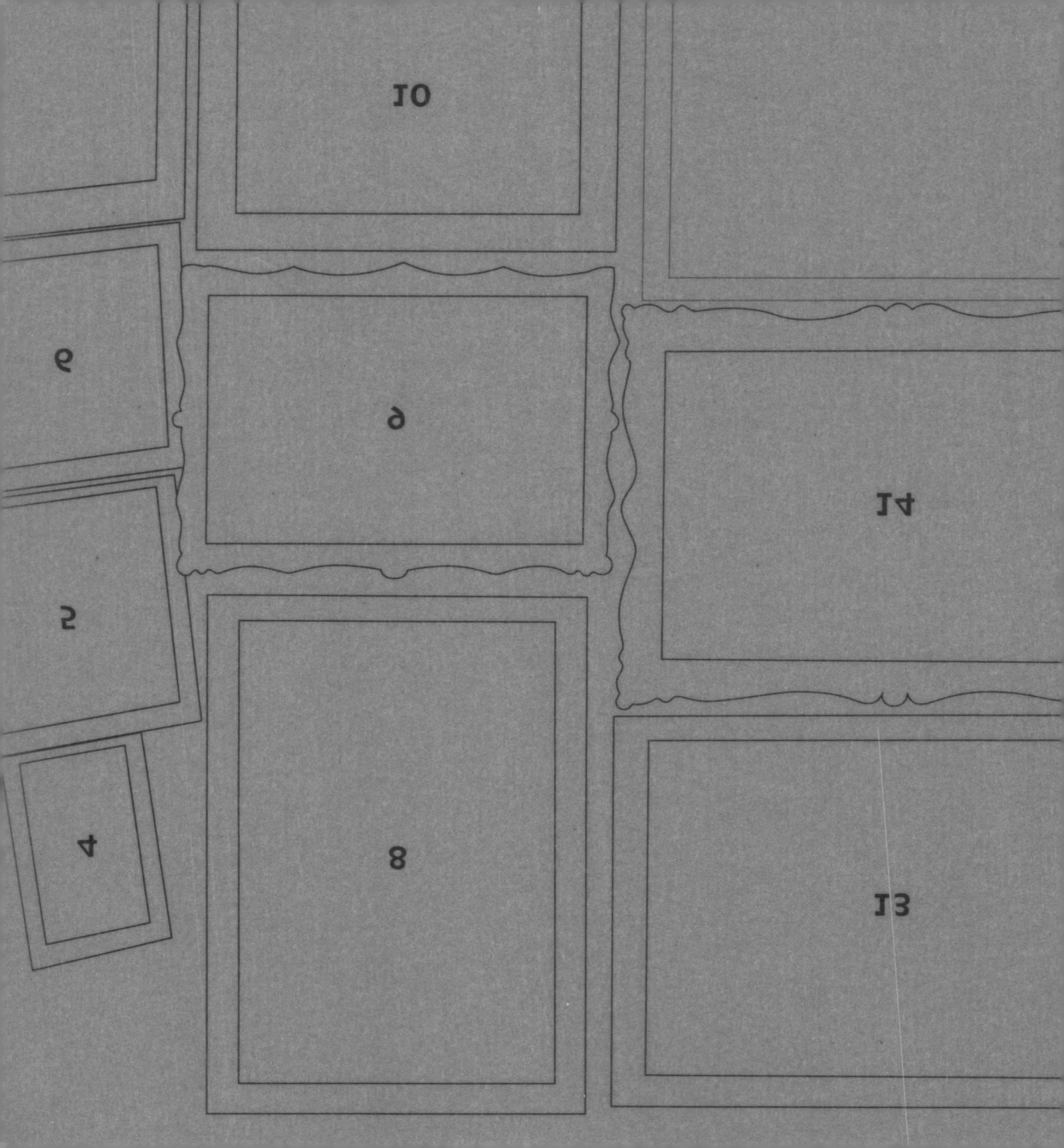

15 Cornelis Huysmans (1648–1727, Flemish), *Landscape with Shepherds and Herd*

16 Anthony van Dyck (1599–1641, Flemish), *Portrait of a Lady and Her Daughter*

22 Peter Paul Rubens (1577–1640, Flemish), *Lot and His Family Fleeing Sodom*

23 Claude Gelée, known as Claude Lorrain (c. 1602–1682, French), *Sunset at the Harbor*

26 Salvator Rosa (1615–1673, Italian), *Landscape with Soldiers and Hunters*

27 Raffaello Santi, known as Raphael (1483–1520, Italian), *Madonna and Child with the Infant Saint John the Baptist*, called *La Belle Jardinière*

28 Anthony van Dyck (1599–1641, Flemish), *Portrait of a Man in Black* (the artist Paul de Vos?)

17 Titian (Italian, 1488/89–1576). *Francis I*, 1539. Oil on canvas, 45¹⁵⁄₁₆ × 35¹⁄₁₆ in. (109 × 89 cm). Musée du Louvre, Paris, inv. 753

21 Correggio (Italian, ca. 1489–1534). *Mystic Marriage of Saint Catherine of Alexandria with Saint Sebastian*, 1526–27. Oil on wood, 41⁵⁄₁₆ × 40³⁄₁₆ in. (105 × 102 cm). Musée du Louvre, Paris

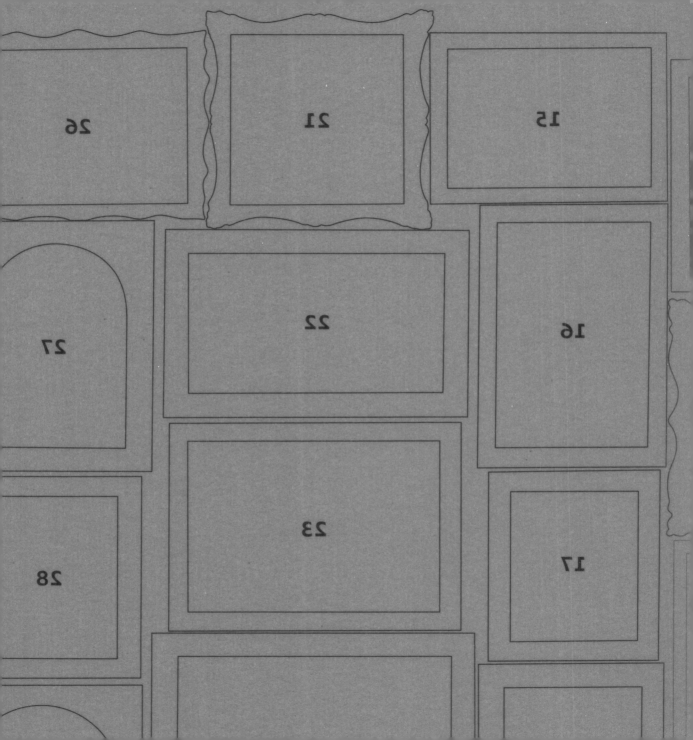

ART

27 Raffaello Santi, known as Raphael (1483–1520, Italian), *Madonna and Child with the Infant Saint John the Baptist*, called *La Belle Jardinière*

28 Anthony van Dyck (1599–1641, Flemish), *Portrait of a Man in Black* (the artist Paul de Vos?)

32 Rembrandt Harmensz van Rijn (1606–1669, Dutch), *Head of an Old Man*

33 Anthony van Dyck (1599–1641, Flemish), *Jesus with the Woman Taken in Adultery*

34 Joseph Vernet (1714–1789, French), *Marine View by Moonlight*

35 Guido Reni (Italian, 1575–1642). *Deianeira Abducted by the Centaur Nessus*, 1617–21. Oil on canvas, 37¹/₁₆ × 29¹⁵/₁₆ in. (94.1 × 75.9 cm). Musée du Louvre, Paris, inv. 537

36 Peter Paul Rubens (Flemish, 1577–1640). *Tomyris, Queen of the Scyths, Ordering the Head of Cyrus Lowered into a Vessel of Blood*, ca. 1620–25. Oil on canvas, 103⁹/₁₆ × 78³/₈ in. (263 × 199 cm). Musée du Louvre, Paris, inv. 1768

29 Guido Reni (Italian, 1575–1642). *The Union of Design and Color*, ca. 1620–25. Oil on canvas, diameter: 47⅝ in. (121 cm). Musée du Louvre, Paris

40 *Artemis with a Doe*, called *Diana of Versailles*. Roman copy after Greek original attributed to Leochares (4th century BC, Greek). Marble, h. 78¾ in. (200 cm). Musée du Louvre, Paris, MA 589

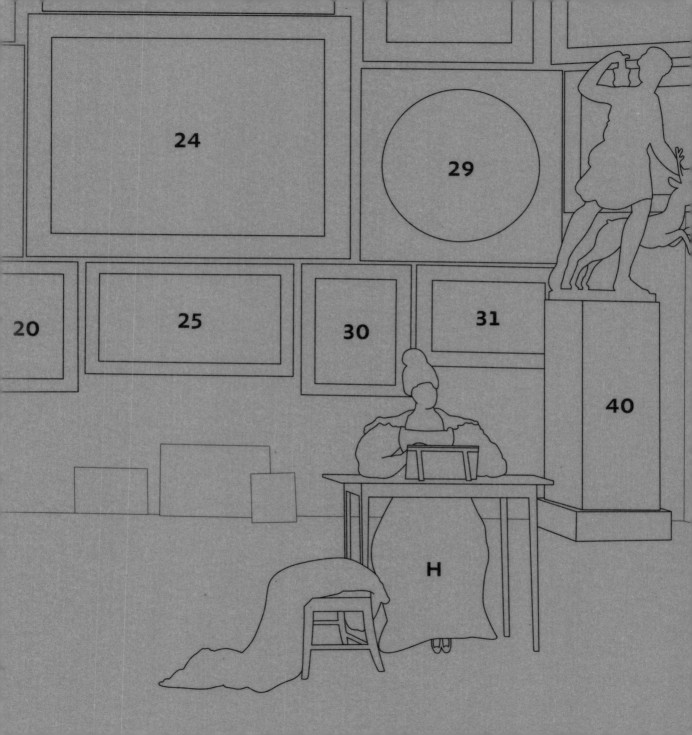

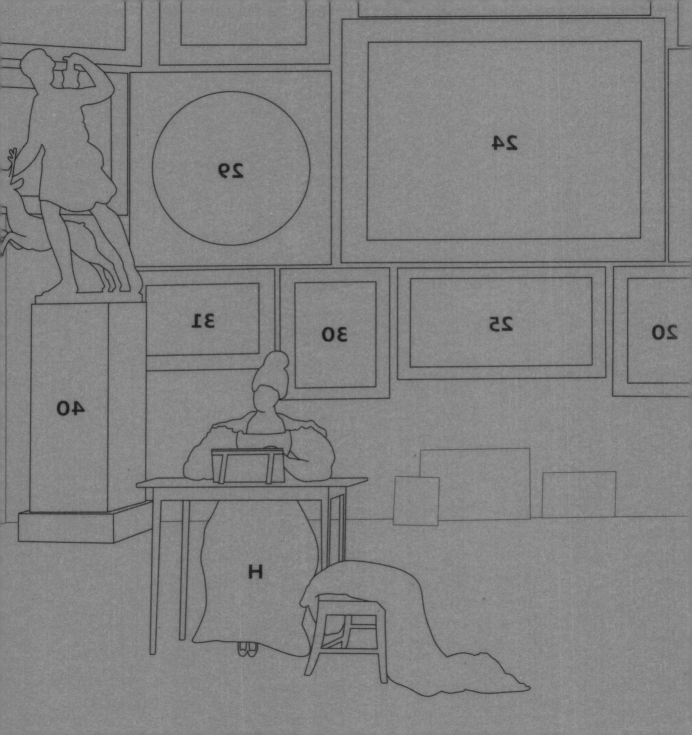

Further Reading

Samuel Finley Breese Morse Papers, 1793–1944. Manuscript Division, Library of Congress, Washington, D.C., http://www.loc.gov/collection/samuel-morse-papers/.

Morse, Samuel F. B. *Lectures on the Affinity of Painting with the Other Fine Arts.* 1826. Edited by Nicolai Cikovsky, Jr. Columbia: University of Missouri Press, 1983.

Brownlee, Peter John, ed. *Samuel F. B. Morse's "Gallery of the Louvre" and the Art of Invention.* Chicago: Terra Foundation for American Art, distributed by Yale University Press, 2014.

Johnston, Patricia. "Samuel F. B. Morse's *Gallery of the Louvre*: Social Tensions in an Ideal World." In *Seeing High and Low: Representing Social Conflict in American Visual Culture*, edited by Patricia Johnston, 42–65. Berkeley: University of California Press, 2006.

Kennedy, Elizabeth, and Olivier Meslay, ed. *American Artists and the Louvre.* Chicago: Terra Foundation for American Art; Paris: Musée du Louvre, 2006. Published in French as *Les artistes américains et le Louvre.* Paris: Hazan, 2006.

Kloss, William. *Samuel F. B. Morse.* New York: Harry N. Abrams in association with the National Museum of American Art, Smithsonian Institution, 1988.

McCullough, David. *The Greater Journey: Americans in Paris.* New York: Simon and Schuster, 2011.

Silverman, Kenneth. *Lightning Man: The Accursed Life of Samuel F. B. Morse.* New York: Alfred A. Knopf, 2003.

Staiti, Paul J. *Samuel F. B. Morse.* Cambridge: Cambridge University Press, 1989.

Photography Credits

This book accompanies the exhibition *Samuel F. B. Morse's "Gallery of the Louvre" and the Art of Invention*, presented at:

The Huntington Library, Art Collections, and Botanical Gardens (San Marino, CA)
January 24, 2015–Monday, May 4, 2015

Amon Carter Museum of American Art (Fort Worth, TX)
May 23, 2015–August 23, 2015

Seattle Art Museum (Seattle, WA)
October 1, 2015–January 10, 2016

Crystal Bridges Museum of American Art (Bentonville, AR)
January 23, 2016–April 18, 2016

Detroit Institute of Arts (Detroit, MI)
June 18, 2016–September 18, 2016

Peabody Essex Museum (Salem, MA)
October 8, 2016–January 8, 2017

Reynolda House Museum of American Art (Winston-Salem, NC)
February 16, 2017–June 4, 2017

New Britain Museum of American Art (New Britain, CT)
June 17, 2017–October 15, 2017

Iris & B. Gerald Cantor Center for Visual Arts at Stanford University
(Stanford, CA)
November 15, 2017–March 18, 2018

Published by the Terra Foundation for American Art
© 2014 Terra Foundation for American Art

Terra Foundation for American Art
120 East Erie Street
Chicago, Illinois 60611
www.terraamericanart.org

Library of Congress Cataloging-in-Publication Data
Terra Foundation for American Art.
 Samuel F.B. Morse's "Gallery of the Louvre": a guide to the painting / Peter John Brownlee.
   pages cm
 ISBN 978-0-692-21294-3 (alk. paper)
 1. Morse, Samuel Finley Breese, 1791-1872. Gallery of the Louvre.
 2. Terra Foundation for American Art. I. Brownlee, Peter John, editor. II. Title.
 ND237.M75A65 2014
 759.13--dc23   2014017411

Produced by Marquand Books, Inc., Seattle
www.marquandbooks.com

Edited by Nancy Grubb and Mariah Keller
Designed by Susan E. Kelly and Ryan Polich
Jacket design by Ryan Polich
Proofread by Sharon Rose Vonasch
Typeset in Whitman and Metro Nova by Brielyn Flones
Color management by iocolor, Seattle
Printed and bound in China by Artron Color Printing Co., Ltd.

Jacket image: Samuel F. B. Morse (American, 1791–1872).
Gallery of the Louvre, 1831–33 [detail]; oil on canvas, 73¾ × 108 in.
(187.3 × 274.3 cm). Terra Foundation for American Art,
Chicago, Daniel J. Terra Collection, 1992.51

TERRA
FOUNDATION FOR AMERICAN ART